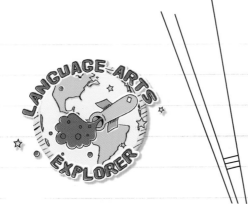

LANGUAGE ARTS EXPLORER

TECHNOLOGICAL DESIGN

by Lyn A. Sirota

SCIENCE LAB:
TECHNOLOGICAL DESIGN

CHERRY LAKE PUBLISHING • ANN ARBOR, MICHIGAN

CHERRY LAKE

Publishing

Published in the United States of America
by Cherry Lake Publishing
Ann Arbor, Michigan
www.cherrylakepublishing.com

Printed in the United States of America
Corporate Graphics Inc
September 2011
CLFA09

Consultants: Heather Abushanab, adjunct professor, Wentworth Institute of Technology; Gail Saunders-Smith, associate professor of literacy, Beeghly College of Education, Youngstown State University

Editorial direction:
Lisa Owings

Book design and illustration:
Kazuko Collins

Photo credits: Shutterstock Images, cover, 1, 18; Ben Blankenburg/iStockphoto, 5; iStockphoto, 7, 16 (bottom); Jonathan Maddock/iStockphoto, 8; Levent Konuk/Shutterstock Images, 11; Sekulovski Ivo/Shutterstock Images, 13; Ana Abejon/iStockphoto, 14; Eduardo Leite/iStockphoto, 16 (top); Yoshikazu Tsuno/AFP/Getty Images, 22; Ewing Galloway/Photolibrary, 23; AP Images, 24; Shuzuo Kambayashi/AP Images, 27

Library of Congress Cataloging-in-Publication Data
Sirota, Lyn A., 1963-
 Science lab. Technological design / by Lyn A. Sirota.
    p. cm. – (Language arts explorer. Science lab)
 Includes bibliographical references and index.
 ISBN 978-1-61080-208-6 – ISBN 978-1-61080-297-0 (pbk.)
 1. Technology–Juvenile literature. 2. Engineering design–Juvenile literature. I. Title. II. Title: Technological design.
 T48.S58 2011
 620'.0042–dc22

                                           2011015640

Cherry Lake Publishing would like to acknowledge the work of The Partnership for 21st Century Skills. Please visit www.21stCenturySkills.org for more information.

TABLE OF CONTENTS

Your Mission 4

What You Know 4

Microwave Ovens 6

Television 10

Cell Phones 14

Computers 18

Gaming Systems 23

Mission Accomplished! 26

Consider This 26

Glossary 28

Learn More 29

Further Missions 30

Index 31

You are being given a mission. The facts in What You Know will help you accomplish it. Remember the clues from What You Know while you are reading the story. The clues and the story will help you answer the questions at the end of the book. Have fun on this adventure!

Your mission is to explore the many aspects of technological design. How and why are different products designed? Why are products changed? How do engineers develop and test new products? Find out about new and future technology. Keep in mind What You Know as you explore the process of technological design.

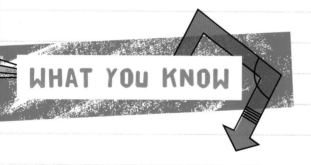

WHAT YOU KNOW

★ Technology is developed to solve specific problems.

★ Wherever people are in the world, there is technology.

★ Scientific advances and customer feedback lead to constant changes and improvements in products.

★ Products become outdated very quickly with the introduction of new technology.

Kate Marley is a student visiting technology companies to learn more about the design process. Carry out your mission by going with Kate on her quest.

You use technology every day. What technological designs do you enjoy using the most?

Today I'm exploring microwave ovens at Whirlwave, Inc. I read a handout from the receptionist while I wait in the lobby. I learn that microwave ovens are named for the waves of energy they use to heat food.

What makes microwave ovens different from regular ovens? I wonder. Just then, Devan Lately comes up and shakes my hand. He is the design team leader at Whirlwave. I figure he is a good person to ask.

"A traditional oven has to heat the air around the food, cooking it from the outside in," Mr. Lately explains. "But a microwave oven heats the water molecules inside the food." He says people like microwave ovens because they can cook food quickly. They are especially good at reheating

MICROWAVE MAGIC

In the 1940s, Dr. Percy Spencer discovered that microwaves could cook food. He was in the lab doing research on microwaves, and he found that the chocolate bar in his pocket had melted. To test his hypothesis that the microwaves were responsible, he held a few popcorn seeds in front of the machine producing the microwaves. The seeds popped, sparking the idea for a microwave oven.

food. And since most of their energy is used to heat the food instead of the oven, microwave ovens use less energy than traditional ovens.

Mr. Lately tells me the first microwaves that came out in the 1950s were almost as big as refrigerators and could cost as much as a car. They weren't very popular.

People became busier in the 1970s and 1980s. They wanted faster ways to cook. Design engineers found ways to make the microwave oven smaller and less expensive, and it became a perfect solution to this problem.

"Is there any reason people wouldn't want to use microwave ovens?" I ask.

Microwave ovens can be found in more than 90 percent of homes in the United States.

"Since microwave ovens heat food from the inside," Mr. Lately says, "they don't brown things or make them crispy on the outside like a traditional oven. Microwaves also don't always heat food evenly. Today's microwave ovens have spinning trays to help with this problem. **Sensors** in some microwaves read moisture levels to tell when food is perfectly cooked."

"That must be how my microwave knows when my popcorn is done," I say. I had microwave popcorn last night. I just pushed a button on my microwave and waited for the beep to tell me it was ready. I didn't have to stand and listen to the popcorn popping, and the popcorn wasn't burned

Microwave ovens are easier and safer for kids to use than traditional ovens.

when I took it out. "I also noticed buttons for baked potatoes and beverages," I say.

"Yes! The sensors are designed for the most commonly microwaved foods. They make microwaves easier and faster to use," says Mr. Lately. I learn that because they are so easy to use, microwaves let children help more in the kitchen. Using a microwave is also far safer than cooking on the stove. Since all the heat stays inside the food, there is less chance of getting burned by a hot pan.

"Do you think microwave ovens will replace regular ovens someday?" I ask.

"Well, some newer microwaves have parts that heat the outside of food just enough to brown it," says Mr. Lately. "Foods cooked in these microwaves look, feel, and taste more like foods cooked in traditional ovens. So it may well be that future microwave ovens will be able to do everything regular ovens can do today."

Mr. Lately thinks future kitchens may have several microwaves for preparing large meals. Microwaves might also find their way into bathrooms and laundry rooms to warm towels or dry clothes. Microwaves have been proven to dry clothes faster and at a lower temperature than just blowing hot air on them. "Maybe they will even dry our hair when we come in from outside on a rainy day," I say with a laugh. ★

This morning I am signing in at a company called Techspot Corporation. They specialize in making televisions. I'm excited to learn more about changes in television technology.

Going Digital

Ellen Sweeney is the vice president of technology at Techspot. She is my guide today. Ms. Sweeney explains that television changed completely when the US government

PRODUCT TESTING

Max Fernandez tells me how Techspot makes sure their products are high quality. "We check our work through random testing," he says. "For example, when we make new TVs, we randomly choose a few and make sure they work the way they're supposed to. If the ones we test all work, we can assume the rest do as well. But mistakes can happen even with all the checking and testing. Sometimes there is a defective part. When we find a problem with a product we've already sold to customers, we may have to recall it. This means we have to let owners of the product know about the problem, and we need to fix or replace the product."

High-definition images look great on large television screens. Some newer TVs even let you view things in 3-D!

forced the switch from analog to **digital**. "This change created the need for new technology," she says. "Digital technology can handle more information and more detailed images. That means you get a better picture and better sound. You also get more channels with digital television. Cable and **satellite** TV providers have changed to digital. Going digital allows them to **broadcast** in high definition."

"I know a high-definition image looks better, but what does high definition mean?" I ask.

"A high-definition image is clearer, sharper, and brighter. It has a higher **resolution**. If you blow up a regular TV image, it will look blurry. But if you blow up a high-definition image, it still looks clear. This means our customers still get a great picture on big TVs."

I follow Ms. Sweeney over to the high-definition TV they have on display. What I see is super clear. I can even see the pores on the actors' faces! I can see why people enjoy watching high-definition television.

Many Ways to Watch

Most of my friends have cable or satellite TV. Others use the Internet to rent movies or TV shows so they can watch them whenever they want. I ask Ms. Sweeney to tell me more about these technologies.

She says television viewing technology has come a long way. Broadcast television is free, but it offers only a few channels, and they differ between locations. Cable and satellite television came about because people weren't satisfied with what they were watching. They were willing to pay for a wide variety of channels and programs.

People also want more control over when they watch shows. Watching shows online or downloading them to a computer or other device lets people watch what they want on their own schedule. People with busy schedules can also use digital video recorders (DVRs) to record shows and even skip commercials.

Many music players can also play video. This let's you watch your favorite shows or movies anywhere.

New viewing technologies allow people to also choose where to watch their favorite shows. Many Techspot customers have home theaters with comfortable chairs and large screens. Others prefer to watch shows on their living room TV, their computer, or even their cell phone or music player.

What will television be like ten years from now? I wonder. I guess I'll have to wait to find out. ★

Today nearly everyone has a cell phone. I'm here at Cellbuy Corporation to learn more about cell phone technology. I'm learning the basics with a presentation.

Here are the most important points:

★ Cell phones send and receive signals over **radio waves**. These signals are passed between radio **antennas**. Each cell, or geographic area, has its own antenna.

★ Cellular phones became widely available in the 1980s.

Many people use their cell phones to send text messages to friends and family instead of calling them.

* By 2008, about 90 percent of adults in the United States were using cell phones. Many use their cell phone as their main line.
* Smartphones are like handheld computers. They allow people to check e-mail, store photos, play music, and browse the Internet.

The presentation showed pictures of some of the first cell phones. They looked like gigantic walkie-talkies—big, bulky, and heavy, with long antennas. I look at my own cell phone. It's thin, light, and you can't see the antenna. It even has a mini keyboard I can use to text my friends.

Ebony Wright is the director of product design at Cellbuy. I ask her what is behind all these changes. "Many things can cause changes in product design," she says. "We look at the phones other companies are making and try to make ours different and better. We also pay attention to what customers want. They want cell phones that are easy to use, easy to carry, and that act as all-in-one devices. Most people like to send text messages. Many also want to send and receive e-mails from their phones. They want phones that let them access the Internet. Others want phones that can store and play music and videos. Most cell phones today can also be used as cameras to take pictures."

Cell phone designs have changed a lot over the years. Many of the newest phones are controlled by touching the screen instead of pushing buttons.

Ms. Wright says Cellbuy's engineers are always working to develop new technology. These changes in technology lead to changes in design. For example, if engineers develop a smaller, lighter battery for the phone, the shape and weight of the phone itself will change.

"What are some things we might see in future cell phones?" I ask.

"Smartphones are all the rage right now and will get more and more popular," says Ms. Wright. "Browsing the Internet is easy with a smartphone. Many people use smartphones to update social networks like Facebook and Twitter."

Ms. Wright also tells me future cell phones will take clearer pictures, play videos, offer better games with 3-D graphics, and be able to run many software programs without slowing down.

It seems like cell phones will be able to do just about everything in the future. Wouldn't it be cool if ten years from now, the only electronic device you needed was a cell phone? ★

SIMON SAYS LET'S TALK!

In 1992, IBM came up with an idea for a phone that could help people with office tasks. After careful planning and research, the world's first smartphone was born! IBM named it Simon and released it in 1993 as a cross between a cell phone and a personal digital assistant (PDA). Simon provided phone and e-mail services and helped workers stay organized.

I'm at Compute It, Inc., a company that makes personal computers (PCs). I know computers today are much smaller and faster than ever before. I'm curious what other changes I'll discover here. Molly Atberg, the public relations manager, takes me on a tour.

"Computers store and process information in the form of words, numbers, pictures, and sounds," Ms. Atberg explains as we walk. "Personal computers are designed to be used by one person at a time."

I learn that for most people in the 1970s, the personal computer was a device right out of a science fiction movie.

Laptop computers are small enough to carry with you anywhere. They can let you do your homework outside!

By the late 1990s, PCs were in millions of homes across the United States. They were as common in offices as staplers.

"Everyone I know has access to a computer," I say. "I use the computer for almost all of my schoolwork and projects. What did kids do before computers?"

Ms. Atberg smiles. "It's a different experience today for kids. When I needed a definition, I used a dictionary. If I had to do research for a project, I went to the library to find books on the subject. Computers have become so easy to use that they are great tools for teaching even young children. And the Internet lets students do much of their research online."

The Internet

Ms. Atberg explains that through the invention of the Internet and the World Wide Web, people can find almost any information they need on their computers. The Internet began as a way for scientists and the government to share information in the late 1960s. The network grew to include businesses, and finally everyone else. In 1991, the World Wide Web provided a way to share images and sound as well as text. People could jump from site to site by clicking links. The Net exploded.

I know the Internet is a big part of many people's lives today. All new computers are made to connect to it. Computers have become shopping malls, libraries, recipe books, travel agents, home theaters, and photo albums. The Internet has changed the way we use computers. It has also changed how we communicate and made it super fast and easy to share all kinds of information!

Computer Design

Ms. Atberg tells me all computers have a **microprocessor**. "The microprocessor is the brain of the computer," she says. "It follows instructions and carries out tasks."

"What makes a microprocessor so smart?" I ask.

"It has a chip in it. The chip was made in a clean room—a dust-free environment. Chips today are so tiny and precise that even a few bits of dirt or dust can ruin them. They are constantly being made faster, smaller, and less expensive. These advances allow companies to design faster, smaller, less expensive computers."

Ms. Atberg points to a screen in the office closest to us. "We've talked about computer hardware, but software programs have also changed a lot. Software programs give microprocessors their instructions. It used to be that a computer could only carry out one set of instructions at a time. But changes in software programs allow modern computers to do many different things at once. Software programs let you store data, write reports, make calculations, and even play games," she says.

"Wow, computers can do so much already," I say. "What will they be able to do in the future?"

Ms. Atberg tells me that computer technology advances so quickly that most computers are outdated the moment you buy them. Computing power doubles about every two years! She says many companies today are trying to find ways of making artificial intelligence—computers that think like humans. Some engineers are trying to make machines that do everything humans can

ARTIFICIAL INTELLIGENCE

ASIMO, made by Honda in Japan, is the world's first robot to walk like a human. It can go up and down stairs, step over curbs, and avoid bumping into people. It can also shake hands, recognize people's faces, and respond to basic commands or questions. TOPIO is another advanced robot made by TOSY Robotics in Vietnam. TOPIO is designed to play ping-pong against humans. The more games it plays, the better it gets!

Honda is working on a robot called ASIMO that can move like humans do. ASIMO can also respond to basic questions, commands, and gestures.

do, only better. Someday, they hope there will be little difference between humans and machines. I wonder if this is really possible and what the future would be like with artificial intelligence. For now, I'm happy with all the things my computer at home can do. ★

Today I am meeting with Joan Frank. She is the market research manager of Game On, a company that makes video games.

I know video games have changed a lot, so I ask Ms. Frank to give me a little history. "Back in the day," she says, "arcade games like pinball were popular. They had lots of moving parts—levers, springs, knobs, and balls—that players had to be skilled at controlling to win the game. Later on, early video games like Space Invaders, Pac-Man, and Super Mario Brothers became the favorites."

"How come kids would rather play these games than pinball?" I ask.

By the 1980s, arcades were full of some of the earliest video games.

Some video games with motion sensors help players stay active and fit.

Ms. Frank says a pinball game was always the same, no matter how many times you played it. Video games changed as players got better. They also allowed players to do many different things in one game. PCs made it possible to play video games at home.

Video game controls also became more advanced and easier to use. Players today have controllers with more options. Through motion sensors, they can even use their bodies to control the newest games.

Graphics have changed too. They started out simple and two-dimensional. Customers wanted games to look cool and feel real, so 3-D graphics developed. Plants swayed in the breeze, flowers blossomed, and water rippled. Many video game designers build entire **virtual** worlds for players to explore.

Ms. Frank tells me video games today are even more fun because you can play them with all your friends instead of having to take turns. You can even play games on the Internet with people all over the world.

I ask Ms. Frank what future technologies might make video games even better than they are now.

Ms. Frank says the future of gaming is inside your head. The first brain-computer interface (BCI) device already exists. It lets people play a game using only their thoughts to control it. The BCI fits over your head and uses sensors to measure brain activity. Your brain activity controls the game. In the future, devices like BCIs might let players smell, taste, or feel objects in the virtual world of the game. ★

BETA TESTING

When video game designers are almost finished with a game, they hire people to play it and make sure it does what it is supposed to do. This process is called beta testing, and the people who test the games are called beta testers. That's right—some people get paid to play video games! Beta testing is an important part of technological design. Testers find errors in games and sometimes point out ways to improve them. Without beta testing, products would not work as well as they do.

You're officially a technology guru! You've learned how different technologies are designed and what problems they solve. You've learned that products are changed to fix problems or to introduce new features. You know products have to be tested before they can be sold. You've developed important insights into how technology companies work. You've heard company employees tell you how and why their product designs have changed. Congratulations on a successful mission!

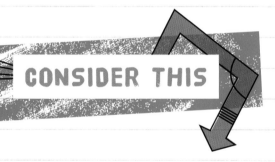

CONSIDER THIS

★ How well do the technological products in your house serve their purposes? How would you change them to make them better?

★ How has the technology in your home changed over the last few years?

★ Would you recommend the products you own to other people? Why or why not?

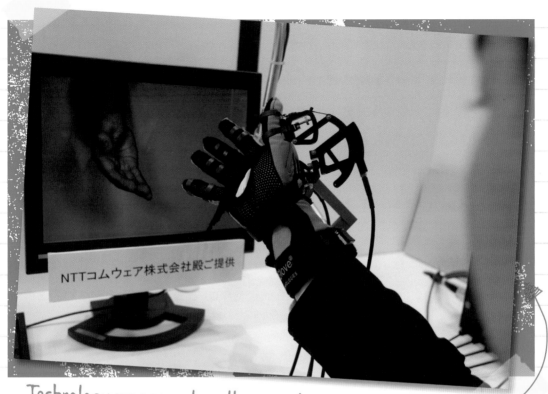

Technology may someday allow people to touch objects in faraway places.

★ What sorts of technology do you think you will own or be using in ten years?

★ What do you think these future products will look like? What new features will they have to offer?

GLOSSARY

antenna (an-TEN-uh) a device for sending or receiving radio or television signals

broadcast (BRAWD-kast) to send out a radio or television program

digital (DIJ-i-tuhl) uses the numbers 0 and 1 to represent text, images, or sound

microprocessor (MYE-kroh-prah-ses-ur) a computer chip that controls the functions of a computer or other electronic device

radio waves (RAY-dee-oh wayvz) electromagnetic waves broadcast from an antenna and used for communication

resolution (rez-uh-LOO-shuhn) the quality of an image; high-resolution images look clear even in large sizes

satellite (SAT-uh-lite) an object put into orbit around Earth to relay information

sensor (SEN-sur) an instrument that can detect and measure changes

virtual (VUR-choo-uhl) made to seem like the real thing through sounds and images

BOOKS

Bailey, Gerry. *Technology*. New York: Gareth Stevens
Publishing, 2009.

Egan, Jill, and Rhea Stewart. *How Video Game Designers
Use Math*. New York: Facts On File, Inc., 2009.

Welsbacher, Anne. *Earth-Friendly Design*. Minneapolis:
Lerner Publishing Group, 2008.

WEB SITES

Explain that Stuff!

http://www.explainthatstuff.com/electricity.html

Explore many different types of electricity on this
site.

PBS Kids Cyberchase

http://pbskids.org/cyberchase

Enter the cyberworld in a fun, safe site.

Science Kids

http://www.sciencekids.co.nz/

Check out this site for science and technology facts
and fun.

BE A PRODUCT DESIGNER

Think of a product you use in your everyday life that doesn't work as well as you'd like it to. Invent an improved product, or even an entirely new one. What would this new product look like? Make a sketch. What special features does it have? Can it perform more than one task? How would you use it? How might other people use it?

MARKET YOUR PRODUCT

Think of a name for your invention. How could you let people know about your product? What might make people want to buy it? How is it different from other products? Would it be expensive to make? What if it didn't work the way people expected it to?

INDEX

antennas, 14–15

artificial intelligence, 21–22

beta testing, 25

brain-computer interface
   (BCI), 25

broadcast, 11, 12

cell phones, 13, 14–17

chips, 20

development, 4, 16, 24

digital technology, 10–11, 12,
   17

energy, 6–7

engineers, 4, 7, 16, 21

high definition, 11–12

Internet, 12, 15, 17, 19–20,
   25

microprocessors, 20

microwave ovens, 6–9

personal computers (PCs),
   12–13, 14, 18–22

product testing, 4, 6, 10, 25,
   26

radio waves, 14

resolution, 11–12

satellite television, 11, 12

smartphones, 15, 17

software, 17, 20–21

televisions, 10–13

video games, 23–25

virtual worlds, 24–25

ABOUT THE AUTHOR

Lyn Sirota's publishing credits include more than 15 nonfiction books. Sirota has numerous articles and poems in popular children's magazines and is a regular contributor to *Science Weekly*. She is a graduate of the Institute of Children's Literature and holds a master's degree in industrial psychology.

ABOUT THE CONSULTANTS

Heather Beck Abushanab has a PhD in mechanical engineering from MIT. She currently works as an adjunct professor at Wentworth Institute of Technology in Boston, MA, in the Applied Math and Sciences Department. She lives in Framingham, MA, with her husband and two children.

Gail Saunders-Smith is a former classroom teacher and Reading Recovery teacher leader. Currently she teaches literacy courses at Youngstown State University in Ohio. Gail is the author of many books for children and three professional books for teachers.